# 20 THINGS YOU DIDN'T KNOW ABOUT SPIDERS

DID YOU KNOW? BUGS



DOUG BRADLEY

PowerKiDS press

Published in 2027 by The Rosen Publishing Group, Inc.
2544 Clinton Street, Buffalo, NY 14224



Portions of this work were originally authored by Therese Shea and published as *20 Fun Facts About Spiders*. All new material in this edition was authored by Doug Bradley.

Editor: Greg Roza
Book Design: Michael Flynn

Photo Credits: Cover Tran The Ngoc/Shutterstock.com; series background freshcare/Shutterstock.com; p. 4 Life on white/Alamy; p. 5 Allen Creative/Steve Allen/Alamy; p. 6 blickwinkel/Hecker/Alamy; p. 8 Lukas Jonaitis/Shutterstock.com; p. 9 Konstantin Andreev/Alamy; p. 10 photobar/Shutterstock.com; p. 11 Alex Stemmer/Shutterstock.com; p. 12 Norbert Dr. Lange/Alamy; p. 13 Adeel Ahmed photos/Shutterstock.com; p. 14 Jason Bazzano/Shutterstock.com; p. 15 Marek Stefunko/Shutterstock.com; p. 16 https://commons.wikimedia.org/wiki/File:Australian_garden_orb_weaver_spider_spinneret.jpg; p. 17 Edijs K/Shutterstock.com; p. 18 Manoj kumar Tuteja/Alamy; p. 19 zaidi razak/Shutterstock.com; p. 20 Paul Harrison/Alamy; p. 21 Malcolm Schuyl/Shutterstock.com; p. 22 Antje Schulte - Spiders and Co./Alamy; p. 23 Vinícius Souza/Alamy; p. 24 Milan Zygmunt/Shutterstock.com; p. 25 Catherine Hoggins/Shutterstock.com; p. 26 Colin Marshall/Alamy; p. 27 Bryan Reynolds/Alamy; p. 28 Pong Wira/Shutterstock.com; p. 29 Jay Ondreicka/Shutterstock.com.

Cataloging-in-Publication Data

Names: Bradley, Doug, 1971-.
Title: 20 things you didn't know about spiders / Doug Bradley.
Description: Buffalo, New York : PowerKids Press, 2027. | Series: Did you know? bugs | Includes glossary and index.
Identifiers: ISBN 9781499457452 (pbk.) | ISBN 9781499457469 (library bound) | ISBN 9781499457476 (ebook)
Subjects: LCSH: Spiders--Juvenile literature.
Classification: LCC QL452.2 B656 2027 | DDC 595.44 -dc23

Printed in China



CPSIA Compliance Information: Batch #QSPK27. For Further Information contact Rosen Publishing at 1-800-237-9932.

# CONTENTS

# CREEPY OR COOL?

Spiders are everywhere! You'll find them in city parks, country fields, and even your house! Most people know they have many legs and use webs to catch insects. You might even know that many spiders are **venomous**, though only a few could harm people.

There are about 42,000 **species** of spiders, and they all differ in some way. Many people find spiders creepy or gross, but the more you read about them, the more you'll realize what amazing creatures they are.

Spiders live almost everywhere on Earth, except Antarctica.

# AWESOME ARACHNIDS

## FACT 1

**MANY PEOPLE THINK SPIDERS ARE INSECTS, BUT THAT'S NOT TRUE.**

Spiders aren't insects. They're **arachnids**. While insects usually have wings, arachnids don't. Their bodies are divided into two parts, while insects have three. Arachnids have eight legs, not six. Arachnids also don't have feelers, or antennae, as insects do.

The two main parts of a spider's body are the abdomen (stomach) and the cephalothorax (head and torso).

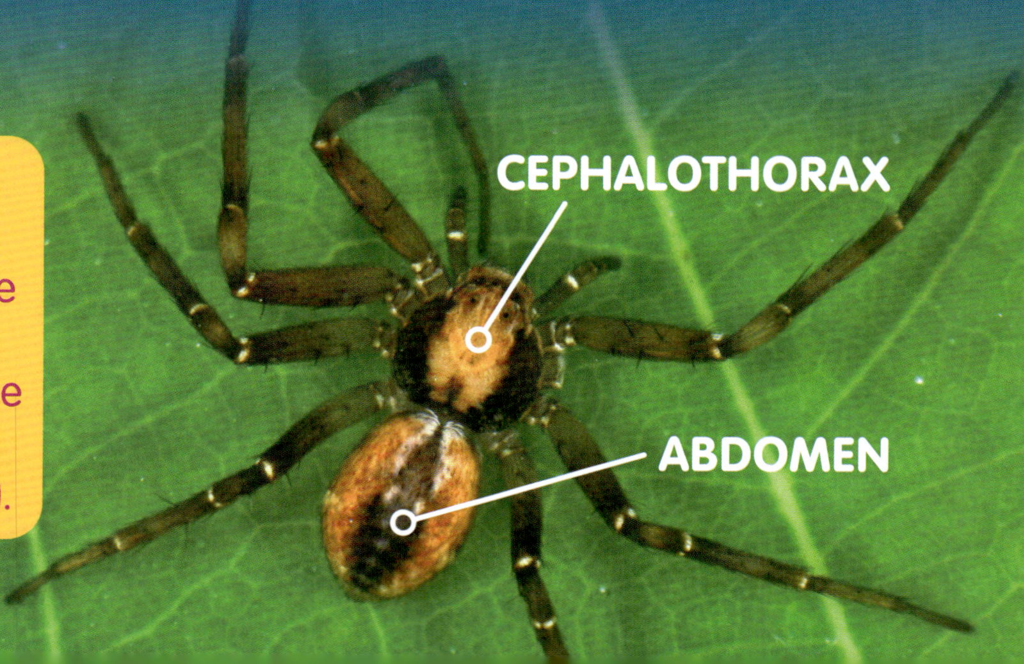

# COMPARING ARACHNIDS AND INSECTS

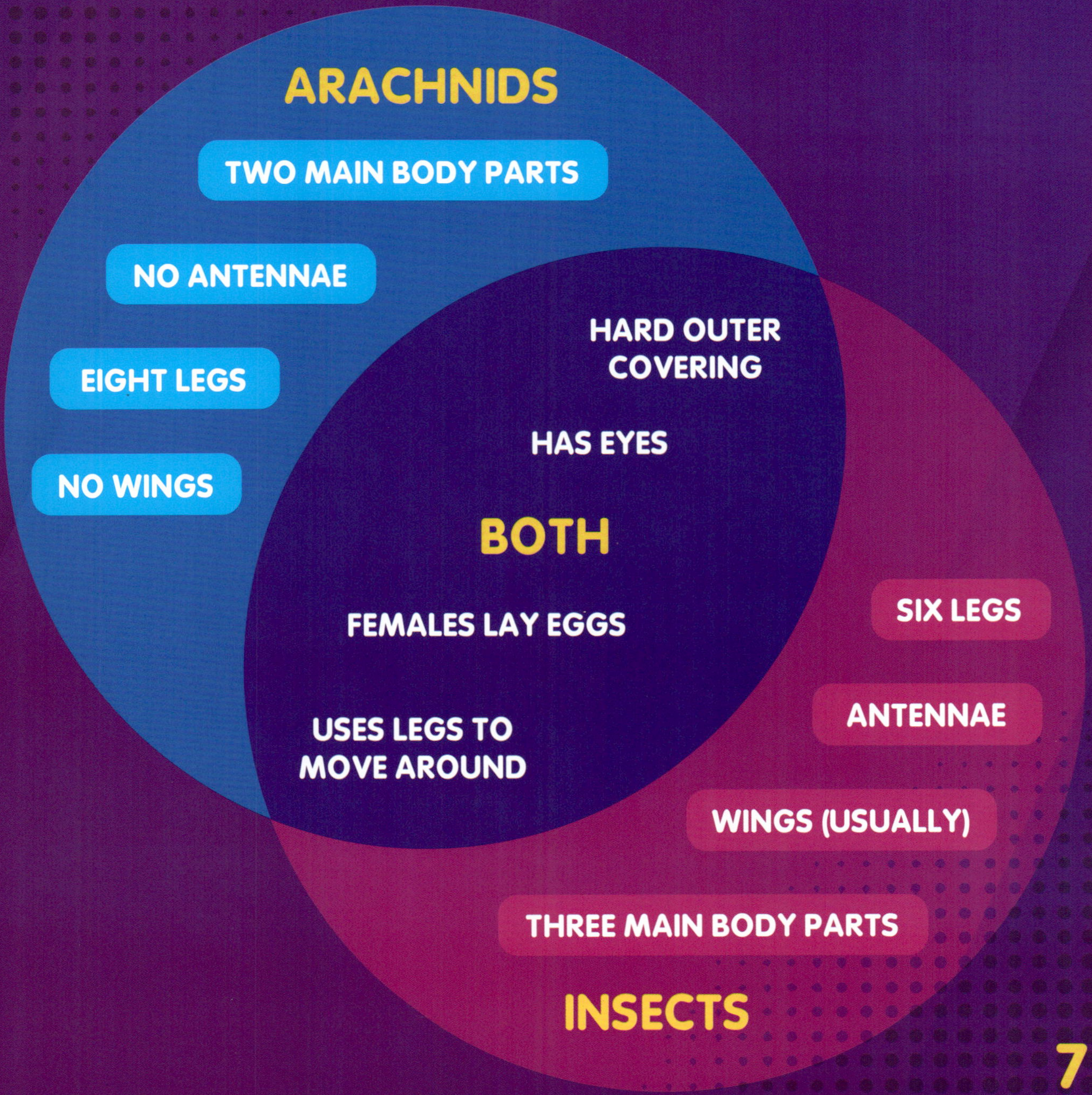

# SPIDER SENSES

## FACT 2

**MOST SPIDERS HAVE EIGHT EYES. SOME SPIDERS HAVE NO EYES.**

Some spiders have two, four, or six eyes. Most spiders have eight eyes arranged in pairs on their head. But others have none! These spiders live in dark places such as caves. Eyes wouldn't help them find food there.

Nearly all spider species have eight eyes. Most of the rest have six eyes.

Jumping spiders sit very still as prey approaches them. Then they use their excellent eyesight to jump at and capture prey.

## SOME SPIDERS HAVE VERY GOOD EYESIGHT, WHILE OTHERS HAVE POOR EYESIGHT.

## FACT 3

Jumping spiders and wolf spiders are types of hunting spiders. They have excellent eyesight. They need it to spot **prey**. Web-building spiders often have poor eyesight. Luckily, they just need to feel prey moving in their webs to catch them. They may see changes in light, though.

## FACT 4

## SPIDERS DON'T HAVE NOSES, BUT THEY CAN SMELL WITH THEIR LEGS.

Spider legs allow a spider to move around, but they're also used to sense the world around them. Each leg is covered with special hairs that can feel **vibrations**. Movements of prey cause vibrations on the ground and in a spider's web. Other leg hairs actually sense smells in the air!

Tarantulas use the hairs on their body for many reasons, including sensing the world around them. When they feel threatened, they can actually fling spiky hairs (sometimes called **nettles**) that cause redness, swelling, and pain.

# SPIDER BODIES

**SPIDERS HAVE MOUTHPARTS THAT OFTEN LOOK LIKE TWO MORE LEGS.**

**FACT 5**

Pedipalps look like legs, but they're not. They are attached to each side of a spider's mouth. Pedipalps have special hairs that sense smells too. Some spiders use them to hold prey. Parts of the pedipalps help some spiders crush food.

Pedipalps look like legs, but they work like a pair of arms and a nose!

## FACT 6

## SPIDERS USE THEIR MOUTH TO EAT, BUT NOT TO BREATHE.

Some spiders breathe through air tubes called tracheae (TRAY-kee-ee). Air enters a spider's tracheae through tiny holes in its body called spiracles. Other spiders have book lungs, which look somewhat like the pages of a book.

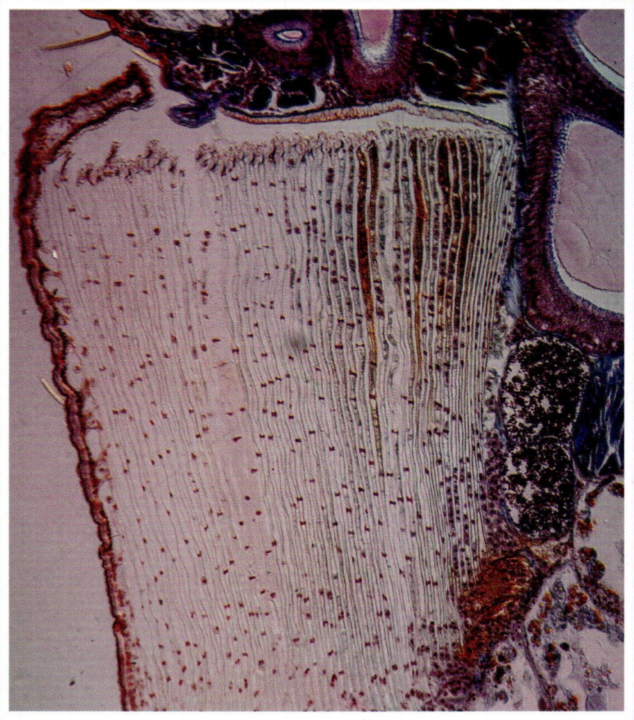

This is what a spider's book lung looks like under a microscope. As a spider's blood runs through book lungs, it trades carbon dioxide for oxygen, just like our lungs do when we breathe.

Tiny spiders make webs to catch prey. Each one is like a work of art.

## FACT 7

## THE SMALLER THE SPIDER, THE MORE SPACE THE BRAIN TAKES UP IN THE BODY.

Small spiders have really, really big brains. Tiny web-spinning spiders have brains so big they spread into their legs! Scientists think a large brain helps a small spider spin its webs as well as large spiders do.

# FACT 8

## SPIDERS USE FANGS AND STRAWS TO EAT.

Spiders grab prey with their chelicerae (kih-LIH-suh-ree). Each of these "jaws" ends in a **fang**. In most spiders, venom travels through the fang. It either **paralyzes** prey or turns its insides to liquid. Then the spider can drink its meal through its straw-like mouth.

When eating, spider fangs come together like pincers. When they feel threatened, a spider may stand on its back legs and spread its fangs wide to scare away attackers.

Fishing spiders trap an air bubble with their legs when diving. This allows them to breathe underwater.

## SOME SPIDERS ARE SO LIGHT THEY CAN WALK ON WATER.

FACT 9

Fishing spiders have long thin legs and light bodies—so light they can walk on water! When they need to hide from **predators**, they dive into water and stay there for over a half hour. Their book lungs get air from bubbles in the water.

# SILKS AND WEBS

## FACT 10

## SPIDERS MAKE DIFFERENT KINDS OF SILK FOR DIFFERENT USES.

Most spiders have different silk **glands** for making different kinds of silk. For example, many female spiders make one kind of silk for weaving webs, another for wrapping eggs, and another for trapping prey.

Spiders spin silk using body parts on their abdomen called spinnerets. Most spiders have six spinnerets.

# SPIDER SILK

| SILK TYPE | USE |
|---|---|
| SWATHING | wrapping prey |
| WEB-MAKING | catching prey |
| DRAGLINE | connecting spider to web in case they fall |
| PARACHUTE/BALLOON | floating on wind to find a new food source |
| SHELTER | making tunnels or nests |
| EGG SAC | keeping eggs safe |
| MATING | males wrap cells to give to female when they **mate** |

## FACT 11

## SOME SPIDERS PREFER TO GO WEBLESS.

Only about half of all spider species spin webs to catch their meals. The rest are hunters. Jumping spiders wait until prey is just a few inches away and then jump on it. However, they can jump more than 40 times the length of their own body!

As the name suggests, huntsman spiders are great hunters.

Trap-door spiders hunt by ambushing prey. That means they hide and wait for prey to walk by, then they attack.

## SOME SPIDERS LIKE TO PLAY HIDE-AND-SEEK WITH THEIR PREY.

**FACT 12**

Trap-door spiders dig their nests in the ground and line them with silk. They make a door out of dirt and silk. They hide inside and when they feel a vibration above, they quickly swing open the door and give their prey a deadly bite.

# SPIDER PARENTS

## FACT 13

**MALE SPIDERS TRY TO IMPRESS FEMALE SPIDERS BY PUTTING ON A SHOW.**

Male spiders will do anything to get the attention of a female when they're ready to mate. Hunting spiders "dance" by waving their legs or stomping on the ground. Jumping spiders show off colorful hairs. Some male nursery-web spiders give females a gift before mating—a silk-wrapped fly.

This species of jumping spider is commonly called a peacock spider. Males display colorful patterns on their abdomens to attract mates, just like peacocks do.

The nursery web spider carries its egg sac around to keep it safe.

## SOME FEMALE SPIDERS LAY A FEW EGGS AT A TIME. OTHERS LAY THOUSANDS OF EGGS!

## FACT 14

Depending on how many eggs they lay, a female spider may put their eggs in a pouch, or sac. They attach the sac to a plant. Some species carry them around. Some spiders' sacs hold hundreds of eggs, and some species of spider make several sacs at one time, resulting in thousands of eggs.

# SPIDERLINGS

## FACT 15

## SOME BABY SPIDERS TRAVEL IN STYLE!

Some young spiders stay near their mother. She helps them find food to eat. Mother wolf spiders carry their spiderlings on their back. Others climb high, spin a long line of silk called a dragline, and let the wind carry them someplace else.

Using a dragline to travel is called "ballooning."

Molting spiders need to wait until their new outer skin, or exoskeleton, has dried.

## YOUNG SPIDERS CAN REGROW A LOST LEG WHEN THEY SHED THEIR OUTER COVERING.

**FACT 16**

As spiderlings grow larger, they molt, or shed their skin. They grow until they burst out of their old skin. This may happen up to 12 times before they're adults. If they lose a leg, they'll grow a new one when they molt!

# SIZING THINGS UP

## FACT 17

## THE GOLIATH BIRDEATER TARANTULA WOULD FILL UP A DINNER PLATE.

The goliath birdeater tarantula may grow to be 1 foot (30.5 cm) across! It got its name because someone reported seeing one eat a bird. This tarantula's fangs can be 1 inch (2.5 cm) long. It lives in South American rainforests.

The goliath tarantula makes hissing sounds, unlike most spiders.

The Patu digua spider could stand on a pinhead.

## A DINNER PLATE COULD HOLD HUNDREDS OF THE SMALLEST SPECIES OF SPIDER.

FACT 18

Many people think the male Patu digua spider is the smallest spider in the world. (Male spiders are usually smaller than females of the same species.) The Patu digua measures just 3/200 inch (0.38 mm)! It can be found on the Southeast Asian island of Borneo.

# PREDATORS

## FACT 19

## SPIDER WASPS ARE THE SPIDER'S WORST ENEMIES.

Spider wasps sting spiders, sometimes killing them and sometimes paralyzing them. Then they bring the spider to their young as a meal. Spider wasps will pick fights with much larger spiders.

This spider wasp has caught a spider for dinner!

Much like trap-door spiders, assassin bugs are excellent at ambushing their prey.

## SOME PREDATORS PRETEND TO GET CAUGHT IN SPIDERWEBS.

**FACT 20**

Spider predators include lizards, snakes, frogs, and fish. One clever enemy—the **assassin** bug—pretends to get caught in a spider's web. When the spider feels its vibration, it runs over to bite it. Instead, the assassin bug kills the spider!

# NOT SO CREEPY AFTER ALL!

A very small number of spider species can harm people with their venom. In North America, this includes the black widow and the brown recluse. However, even these spiders would rather run away than bite.

A single spider eats about 2,000 insects a year. These are insects that could otherwise be running around your house! Even more helpful are spiders that kill grasshoppers and other pests that eat the crops we depend on for food. So maybe spiders aren't so bad after all!

BROWN RECLUSE

The black widow and the brown recluse are the most venomous spiders in North America.

# GLOSSARY

**arachnid:** One of a large class of small animals that includes spiders, scorpions, ticks, daddy longlegs, and mites.

**assassin:** Someone or something that kills with a sudden attack.

**fang:** A long, pointed tooth.

**gland:** A body part that produces something needed for a bodily function.

**mate:** One of two animals that come together to produce babies. Also to come together to make babies.

**nettle:** Any of several tall plants with stinging hairs on the leaves and stems.

**paralyze:** To make something lose the ability to move.

**predator:** An animal that hunts other animals for food.

**prey:** An animal that is hunted by other animals for food.

**species:** A group of animals that are all of the same kind.

**venomous:** Able to produce a liquid called venom that is harmful to other animals.

**vibration:** A rapid movement back and forth.

# FOR MORE INFORMATION

## BOOKS

Klepeis, Alicia Z. *Peacock Spiders*. Bloomington, MN: Pogo, 2026.

Owen, Ruth. *Spiders: We're Not Scary, We're Amazing!* Kent, UK: Ruby Tuesday Books, 2023.

## WEBSITES

**Black Widow**
*kids.nationalgeographic.com/animals/invertebrates/facts/black-widow*
Learn all about the venomous black widow spider at National Geographic Kids.

**How Spiders Work**
*science.howstuffworks.com/environmental/life/zoology/insects-arachnids/spider.htm*
Learn more about spider parts and why they're some of the coolest animals on Earth.

# INDEX